School in a valley

Mary Hill

Contents

1	The country of Wales	2
2	The town of Dolgellau	3
3	A river valley	6
4	How valleys and lakes were formed by glaciers	10
5	The weather	12
6	The position of the school	14
7	How the children get to school	16
8	The design of the school	18
9	The Welsh language	20
10	The school day and after-school clubs	25
11	What the children eat	26
12	School outings	27
13	Festivals	28
14	Outings to the Snowdonia National Park	30
	Glossary	31
	Further information	32
	Index	33

1 The country of Wales

Wales is a mountainous country. On three sides the sea laps its shores. On its border to the east is England.

Wales is very beautiful, and many tourists visit it. They go to walk in the high mountains and green valleys. Some go to fish in the rivers, or to visit seaside towns like Barmouth. In the north of Wales there is the Snowdonia National Park.

This book is about life in a town called Dolgellau in Wales and in the primary school there.

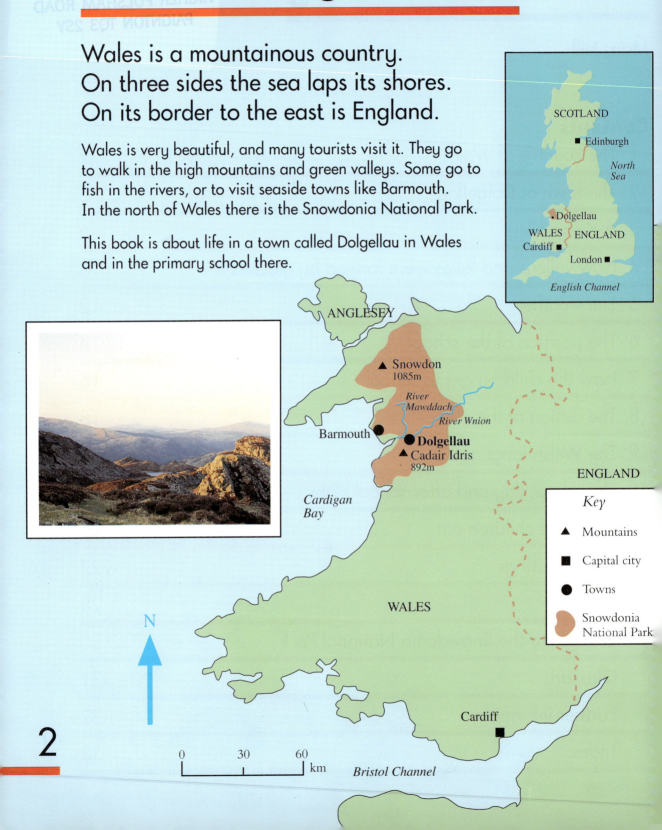

2 The town of Dolgellau

Dolgellau (pronounced Dol-geth-lie) is a small market town. It lies in a mountain valley in the Snowdonia National Park.

Hundreds of years ago people found Dolgellau a good place to live, so they made a town there. The mountains gave shelter from the winds and provided stone to build houses and slate for roofs. The rivers provided water. The people travelled along the river valleys.

There is one primary school in Dolgellau, called Ysgol Gynradd Dolgellau. There is also a comprehensive school.

 The main road follows the path of the river.

 Dolgellau town centre.

What Dolgellau is like

Dolgellau has a population of nearly 3000 people. The centre of the town has narrow twisting streets. There are small shops with homes above them. A large supermarket has been built just outside the town.

Tourists visit Dolgellau, because it is situated in beautiful countryside. They like to climb up Cadair Idris and other mountains. The sea is only thirteen kilometres away in Cardigan Bay.

Farming in the valley

Dolgellau is surrounded by mountains. The soil on top of these mountains is thin and the grass is poor, but sheep can graze there in summer. In winter, farmers bring the sheep to fields lower down the mountains where the grass is better. In bad weather the sheep can be given hay and cattle cake.

Sheep and cattle are sold in the livestock market in Dolgellau.

Farmers from miles away send their sheep to this important market.

3 A river valley

A valley is the low land between hills and mountains. A stream or river usually flows through it. Rivers start high in the mountains and flow down to the sea.

Some valleys are formed by rivers. These valleys are narrow and v-shaped, and their sides are rough and sloping. Millions of years ago water, ice and wind wore away parts of the mountains. The rain made channels in the rocks.

River runs along valley bottom

Rivers form v-shaped valleys.

The upper part of a river valley

At the top of a Welsh mountain the water runs down fast. The force of the water knocks out large stones and pebbles. This makes the channels bigger. Many valleys are formed in this way by erosion of the land.

The middle part of a river valley

As the water reaches flatter land near Dolgellau, it does not flow so fast. It no longer moves big stones, but it wears away the river banks. When water moves slowly, the sand and gravel that it carries sink to the bottom of the river.

Upper part of a river valley.

After heavy rainfall the mountain streams run faster.

The lower part of the river valley

Dolgellau is built in the lower part of the river valley where the water flows more slowly. To the west of Dolgellau the River Wnion flows into the River Mawddach. Thirteen kilometres downstream it then flows into the sea near Barmouth.

On the bank of the river Mawddach to the west of Dolgellau, there is a bird sanctuary. Children can watch the birds from an old railway signal-box. There are mallard and shelduck, and in winter dunlin and oyster-catchers.

 Looking north over Dolgellau. Steep sided fields surround the small town.

 At low tide the river Mawddach flows slowly round sandbanks in the estuary.

The mouth of the river

The place where the river joins the sea is called the mouth. Between Dolgellau and Barmouth there are salt-marshes. At high tide the sea flows back up the estuary. Where the sea and the river meet, the water oozes over the banks and forms a salt-marsh.

Some rivers flow straight into the sea. They do not have salt-marshes. The sand and mud that they carried from the mountains form sandbanks in the mouth of the river.

4 How valleys and lakes were formed by glaciers

Millions of years ago, some valleys were made by glaciers. A glacier is a large mass of ice which moves slowly down a mountainside.

In the ice age, snow filled the valleys. It turned to ice and formed glaciers. As the glaciers melted, they moved slowly down the valleys. Rocks which had been frozen in the ice wore away the valleys. When the ice melted, wide u-shaped valleys were left.

⬆ Sometimes shallow lakes form in glaciated valleys.

Steep rocky sides circle the cwm on Cadair Idris.

Lakes formed by glaciers

Glaciers sometimes pull away part of a mountainside, leaving a great hollow, which looks like an armchair. Water often collects in the hollow and forms a lake. These circular hollows are called corries, or cwms (pronounced cooms) in Wales.

Cadair Idris, which means the Chair of Idris, is supposed to be named after a Welsh giant called Idris. According to legend, he sat in a cwm on the side of the mountain and studied the stars.

5 The weather

In Wales the weather is very changeable. The winters are wet and the summers, like all British summers, are sometimes sunny and sometimes wet.

It is wet in Wales because the wind often blows from the south-west. The air over the Atlantic is moist. The clouds become colder as they rise over the mountains. This makes the water in the clouds condense and fall as rain.

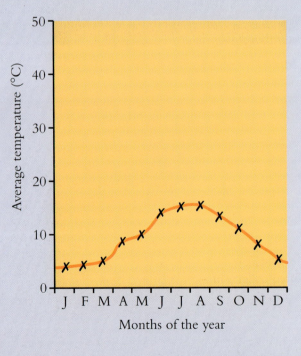

Graph showing average temperatures in Dolgellau.

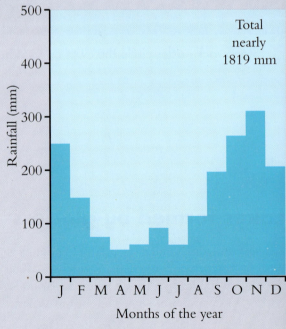

Bar graph showing rainfall in Dolgellau.

The old chimneys in Dolgellau

The old houses in Dolgellau have slate slabs on the sides of the chimneys to stop the rain getting in where the chimney joins the roof. The rain splashes on to the slab and is kept away from the join.

Snow

Little snow falls in Dolgellau. The mountain Cadair Idris is much colder. It gets deep snow which can stay for many days.

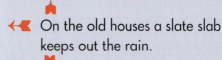

On the old houses a slate slab keeps out the rain.

6 The position of the school

The River Wnion flows through Dolgellau.
The old town is on the south side of the river.
The primary school is built on the newer north side.

The library, the post office, the church and most of the shops are in the old town. When the school was built in 1915, there was no room for it in the old town centre, so it was built on the other side of the river.

⬆ No building is more than four storeys high.

The by-pass

The school is built on the lower slopes of a hill, facing south across the valley. There are few houses on this side of the new by-pass.

The by-pass was built to speed the flow of traffic. It takes vehicles that are not stopping in Dolgellau away from the town centre.

The by-pass was built on the site of an old railway track alongside the river, because this is the flattest part of the valley.

7 How the children get to school

Most of the children live in the newer houses, built on the southern edge of Dolgellau. They walk to school through the old town, but a few are taken to school by car or bus.

Their parents work in the town. Some parents help to look after tourists, while others work at the local government offices or in shops.

Some of the youngest children go to school in a school bus, because it is a long way for them to walk.

Road safety is taught at school.

↑ The youngest children use the school bus which takes them to the town centre.

Going to school by car or taxi

Some parents work in the local government offices, or for the Forestry Commission in the Brenin Forest. They give their children a lift to school in their cars, on their way to work.

A few children live in small villages where the schools are not big enough to provide them with the special help that they need. They come to school by taxi and stay for the mornings only.

8 The design of the school

The school has stone walls and a slate roof. It faces south so that it gets the sun.

The stone and slate used for building the school came from quarries (places where rock is dug out of the mountains). The floors are made of wood, and most of the walls have brown tiles up to shoulder height.

The school has large windows and high ceilings. Two long corridors connect the six classrooms.

Aerial view of the school.

The central hall roof is high and steeply sloping.

↑ The choir practises regularly for the festival.

The rooms in the school

A large room forms the central part of the school, and this is used for school assembly. At other times, it can be made into two rooms, by using a folding screen. There are six classrooms, one of which is used as a music room.

At the back of the building there are cloakrooms and toilets for the children. An office, a staff room and a boiler-room are also at the back of the building.

↑ Using a computer in the assembly hall.

9 The Welsh language

Everyone at the school can speak both Welsh and English. Welsh is an old Celtic language.

The tribes of ancient Britons who lived in England and Wales many centuries ago spoke Welsh.

When the Angles and Saxons invaded England, they made the Britons leave their farms and go west into the hills and mountains of the country which we now call Wales. There the Britons were safe, and they could keep their own language. This language is now called Welsh.

The Welsh have their own television channel instead of Channel 4, and their own radio programmes.

Parking signs in English and Welsh.

↑ Post office notices in English and Welsh.

The Welsh language today

The Saxons called the Britons 'Wealhas', which means strangers. Over the years this changed to Welsh, and the name of the country became Wales.

The Britons called the Saxons 'Saesons'. This is the word that the Welsh still use for English people. The Welsh call their country 'Cymru' and themselves 'Cymry'.

Some words like tomato and banana were originally foreign words, and so they are the same in both English and Welsh.

The Welsh alphabet

There are twenty-eight letters in the Welsh alphabet:

a b c ch d dd e f ff g ng h i l
ll m n o p ph r rh s t th u w y

Some letters sound like the ones in the English alphabet – 'b' as in 'bat', and 'c' as in 'cat'. But many of the letters do not have the same sounds at all.

f = 'v' as in 'have',   dd = 'th' as in 'the',

w = 'oo',   ff = 'f' as in 'for'

Ll is a cross between 's' and 'l', and you blow air out of the corners of your mouth as you say it.

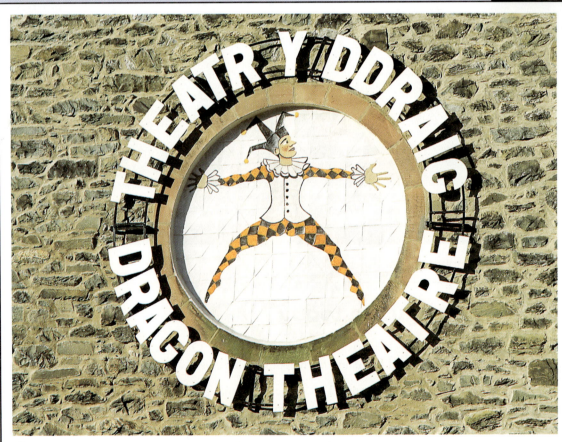

 Public buildings are named in Welsh and English.

 Road markings in Welsh and English.

Some Welsh grammar

When the Welsh describe an object, they put the adjective, the describing word, after the name. So they say 'ci mawr' (= 'dog big'), and 'ci bach' (= 'dog small').

They have two words for 'the' – 'y' is used if the word begins with a consonant: 'y ci' (= 'the dog').
But if the word begins with a vowel, 'yr' is used: 'yr aderyn' (= 'the bird').

The Welsh language in school

Five-year-olds in Dolgellau have most of their lessons in Welsh. They speak Welsh at school even if they do not speak Welsh at home.

As the children get older, they have more lessons in English. By the time that they are ten, they have half their lessons in English and half in Welsh. The children can speak, read, write, and spell in both languages. The children are then bi-lingual, that is, they have two languages.

Everywhere there are signs in English and Welsh.

10 The school day and after-school clubs

The school day is like that of many schools in Wales. After school some children go to clubs.

 The Dolgellau primary school has this timetable.

Time		Lesson/Activity	
9.00 –	9.30 a.m.	Class assembly and reading	
9.30 –	10.30 a.m.	Maths	
10.30 –	10.45 a.m.	Break	
10.45 –	12.00 noon	Themes*	*Themes are subjects like science,
12.00 –	1.00 p.m.	Dinner	religious knowledge and environmental
1.00 –	2.20 p.m.	Themes*	studies.
2.20 –	2.30 p.m.	Break	
2.30 –	3.30 p.m.	Creative activities	
		– PE, art, music, or choir or orchestra practice.	

The Welsh League of Youth

The most popular after-school club is on Thursday, when the Welsh League of Youth meets, this is commonly known as the Urdd. The children can choose to play football, or paint, dance, make music or take part in plays.

11 What the children eat

Most children stay at school for dinner. They can eat in the dining-room, or they can take a packed lunch.

⬆ Eating school lunch ...

or a packed lunch.

When the children go home, they may have a currant bread or Welsh cakes for tea.

Welsh cakes are made with flour, butter, eggs, sugar and currants. They are cooked on a griddle or in a frying pan. They can be eaten hot or cold, with honey, jam or cheese.

Bara Brith is a Welsh bread, made with dried fruit which has been soaked in cold tea.

Favourite Foods

Packed Lunches	School Dinners
cheese sandwiches	pizzas
jam sandwiches	beef burgers and chips
pies	baked beans

12 School outings

Sometimes the pupils go out of school for their lessons. They use maps to find the places that they will visit.

The pupils have visited the Dolgellau livestock market and seen the sheep and cattle being sold.

On one outing the children discovered an ancient spring. Spring water was used in the days before tap water was piped to each home.

 The children watch as the sheep are penned ready for sale.

13 Festivals

On 1st March the Welsh celebrate St David's Day. St David is the patron saint of Wales.

On St David's Day, some people wear a daffodil or a leek, to show their pride in being Welsh. St David, the patron saint of Wales, was a bishop who lived in the sixth century.

The school celebrates St David's Day with a religious service, a concert and a fair.

Statue of St David.

The Dolgellau school orchestra and choir practise regularly and compete at festivals.

Eisteddfod

Welsh people of all ages love music and singing. They enjoy going to an Eisteddfod, which is a gathering where people get together to sing, read poetry, dance and play the Welsh harp.

The children of Dolgellau school take part in the Youth Eisteddfod, which is held in a different part of Wales each year. In 1994 it was held in Dolgellau. These festivals have helped to keep the Welsh language alive. It is a great honour for a poet to be given the title of 'bard' at an Eisteddfod.

⬆ Children come from all over Wales to take part in the Eisteddfod. They dress up or wear school uniform.

14 Outings to the Snowdonia National Park

The Snowdonia National Park is a favourite place for the Dolgellau pupils to go for picnics and walks through the woods and mountains. High stone walls stop sheep from straying.

As Dolgellau is in the National Park, it is a conservation area. No one may change any buildings or cut down any trees without permission. The roofs of houses and offices must be made of slates of the right colour.

The wardens of Snowdonia National Park work hard to conserve the countryside so that people in future years are able to enjoy it.

Glossary

Bard — A bard is a Welsh poet.

By-pass — A by-pass is a road built to take traffic away from the town centre.

Cadair Idris — Cadair Idris is a mountain in Wales, it is 892 metres high.

Cattle cake — Cattle cake is dried food fed to sheep and cattle in the winter.

Celts — Celts were tribes of people living in Britain before the Romans.

Conservation — Conservation means that plants, animals and land or buildings are being protected from damage.

Corry or cwm — A corry or cwm is a hollow left behind after a glacier has taken away some of the rock.

Cymru — Cymru is a Welsh word for Wales. It is pronounced cumree.

Eisteddfod — Eisteddfod is the Welsh festival where people compete in making music, reciting poetry, or drama and other artistic events. It is pronounced eye/steth/fod.

Erosion — Erosion is the wearing away of the land by wind, water or ice.

Dolgellau — Dolgellau is a market town in mid-Wales. It is pronounced Dol/geth/lie.

Glacier — A glacier is a river of slow moving ice. In the Ice Age, there were glaciers in Wales.

Livestock market — A livestock market is where sheep, cattle and other animals are sold.

Marsh — A marsh is where land is very wet because it is often flooded by water.

National Park — A National Park is a large area of countryside which is protected from change or damage.

Snowdonia — Snowdonia is a mountainous area in North Wales. It is named after its highest mountain – Snowdon.

Storey — A storey is a horizontal level of a building.

Valley — A valley is the low land that lies between hills or mountains.

V-shaped valley — A v-shaped valley is formed by a river.

U-shaped valley — A u-shaped valley is formed by a glacier.

Welsh League of Youth — The Welsh League of Youth is a group that helps children have pride in the Welsh way of life.

Further information

Books

Glaciers and Ice Sheets by Gordon de Q Robin, Wayland 1984

Rivers by Terry Jennings, OUP 1986

Rivers and Streams by Mark C. W. Sleep, Wayland 1983

Welsh for Beginners by Angela Wilkes, Usborne 1989

Invaders: Anglo-Saxons and Vikings by Jill Honnywill, Collins 1991

Anglo-Saxon Resource Book by James Mason, Longman 1991

What do we know about the Celts? by Hazel Mary Martell, Simon and Schuster 1993

Museums and places of interest

Wales Information Bureau
The British Travel Centre, 12 Regent Street, London SW1Y 4PQ

Cynor Cefn Gwlad Cymru (Countryside Council for Wales)
Plas Penrhos, Ffordd Penrhos, Bangor, LL57 2LQ

Llyfrgell Genedlaethol Cymru (National Library of Wales)
Penglais, Aberystwyth.

Welsh Folk Museum
St Fapans, Cardiff, CF5 6XB

Amgue-ddfa G. Cymru National Museum of Wales
Cathays Park, Cardiff.

Welsh Education Office
Welsh Office, Government Buildings, Llanishen, Cardiff, CF4 5PL

Snowdonia National Park
National Park Office, Penrhyndendraeth, Gwynedd, LL48 6LS

Cadw-Welsh Historic Monuments
Brunel House, Fitzalan Road, Cardiff, CF2 IUY